Trekking Patagonia: A Guide To Your Own Adventure

By Andy Fine

To Eric and Weldon for gifting me with a deep love for the outdoors, to my parents Michael and Linda for all the travel experiences, and to Willie and Levi for embarking on this incredible adventure with me.

Table of Contents

Introduction

Welcome to A. Fine Adventure's Trekking Patagonia: A Guide to Your Own Adventure. This guide will provide you with imperative insider information to effectively plan and execute your trip to one of the world's greatest treasures. Patagonia is a hiker's dream, full of impressive wilderness with trails to see mesmerizing landscapes worthy of screensavers everywhere. This outdoorsman's utopia comes with many unknowns. When traveling to a new place a world away, you need to be well equipped with insider knowledge to make the most of your time. Advice as to where to go, how long to stay, and all the other logistical considerations involved in planning a trip come at a premium. After a year's worth of planning, two of my best friends and I put our professional lives on hold and set off to trek through Patagonia. In this book, I will share my research and experiences in order to provide you with the insight necessary to plan your own adventure.

I have hiked in the United States, China, Hong Kong, Japan and traveled through Europe, Australia, Thailand, and Vietnam. I can say unequivocally, this three-week trip was the beginning of a love affair with Patagonia I would not trade for anything. You too can be lucky enough to explore this special part of the world. The priceless expansive views, the big sky feeling, and incredible hiking trails made up for all of the confusion and frustration that came along with planning our trip. Through this guide, you will take a ride with me on our trip from the pre-trip planning to the day-to-day adventure. We made mistakes, learned from them, and I hope you can learn from our experiences. The only thing I can guarantee is that even with all the information from every resource available, you will still find unknowns and have to problem solve on the go. My goal is to limit these occurrences for you; after all, why should a problem be solved over and over again?

Traveling is a very personal experience. Everyone has different desires that draw them towards different places and activities. Nevertheless, there will be something here for everyone. My goal is to help you plan a trip similar to ours. However, as the Pre-Trip Planning Guide explains, your own trip will be dependent on your personal goals and interests.

You could certainly spend months or years exploring Patagonia but for us, we had other commitments to return to and three well-planned weeks allowed us time to dive into the highlights of the region including:

- Torres del Paine National Park
- El Calafate
- Los Glaciares National Park
- El Chaltén
- Ushuaia
- Tierra del Fuego National Park

There are plenty of resources available that will complement this guide and give you additional information on lodging, restaurants, and tourist attractions. What is different about this guidebook is the insider information and direction that provides insight into how to trek the region.

Please feel free to reach out to me with any additional questions at andyfineadventure@gmail.com. And finally, enjoy your adventure in Patagonia!

Pre-Trip Planning

When determining an itinerary for any trip, it is important to be self-reflective. Everyone finds enjoyment from different things and chooses to prioritize particular aspects of a trip over others. By identifying what you want out of this adventure, you can design a trip that best fits your ideal vision. For Patagonia, this is essential due to the vast amount of territory covered and variety of attractions and destinations. The following questions will lead you in preparation for your own Patagonia adventure.

How Long Will You Be There?

Trip duration will be chosen based on personal circumstances, desired destinations, and the pace you can handle. Our Patagonia trip was nineteen days including a day at either end for travel from and back to the US. This left us with seventeen travel days in the Patagonia region. We were able to accomplish a great deal in this short period of time, but in hindsight, it would have been helpful to plan a couple extra days to recover physically and not become too exhausted by the end. If you want to spend sufficient time in each location, three to four weeks would be ideal. But those that can spare more time can easily stretch their visit much beyond that.

At the same time, the main attractions of Patagonia could be achieved in as little as ten days if you are extremely pressed for time. Two weeks in Patagonia is still worth it, but you will miss some of what the area has to offer. See suggested Patagonia Itineraries (Page 29) for details on where to go when depending on your duration of stay.

What Type of Traveler Are You?

Especially when choosing companions for a trip, you need to understand what every person is looking for on a trip and the type of traveler each of you is. For example, I know that I am passionate about trekking and other outdoor adventure activities more so than urban exploration. Choosing travel companions to join you on your trip is like choosing a roommate. Even your best friend can make for a terrible roommate. After living together for a month, you learn they have habits and quirks that drive you crazy. Make sure that everyone on the trip has similar goals, expectations, and priorities. When I travel, I prioritize my budget towards food and activities and care less about the quality of lodging. Does this align with you? Or do you hold value for other things? There is no right or wrong answer. Whatever style of traveler you are is okay, but you need to understand what you and your companions want out of the trip so you can design an itinerary that best fits everyone's personality and interests. My companions all had the same desires for our Patagonia adventure: to do a lot of hiking in as many different areas as possible. We thus planned a dense, highly physically intensive trip that was great for us but might need to be adjusted for other travelers.

There are travelers who want every element of the trip to be written in ink and others that value a go-with-the-flow mentality. Having the freedom to see what happens when is part of the fun for some, while the uncertainty can doom others. Knowing where you and your group fall on the spectrum will guide how thorough your trip planning needs to be. Flexibility will be a key determinant of what level of spontaneity can be afforded. With seventeen days on the ground to explore a region that could easily be traveled for three months, a highly specific plan with a day-to-day outline was necessary so we didn't waste time spinning our thumbs and missing out. Bumps in the road are inevitable, and even the most perfect plan will be disrupted by unforetold circumstances, but those armed with the most information will be better set up for a successful trip. And even with all the research and planning you will do, word of mouth from locals and other travelers will likely give you recommendations that cause you to alter the plan unexpectedly. Having an outline is key to give yourself a track to follow, but expect to take some unplanned detours and pit stops along the way. That is all part of the adventure.

Which Destinations Will You Visit?

Only after answering the first two questions can you begin to think about the third. Patagonia is a single term that encompasses an extremely vast range of terrain. Traveling throughout Patagonia takes a lot longer than it appears when looking at a map. How much travel time between locations are you willing to allocate to your trip? Every destination you add to your list increases not just the time there, but the travel time to and from. Cities that appear nearby on a map take at least a two-hour drive, while others take 15-20 hours. The types of activities you are looking for will direct you to certain areas over others. Patagonia offers fantastic trekking opportunities as well as plenty of chances to get immersed in nature, such as penguin tours and boating options. This guide includes information on the highlights of Southern Patagonia we visited including:

- Puerto Natales
- Torres del Paine National Park
- El Calafate
- Los Glaciares National Park-Perito Moreno Glacier
- El Chaltén
- Ushuaia
- Tierra del Fuego National Park

What is the Preferred Mode of Transportation?

Choosing a mode of transportation will be a function of your budget, the nature of the existing infrastructure, and the destinations you wish to reach. In Patagonia, there are two options to consider: public transportation (buses, not trains) and a rental car. The pros and cons are fairly obvious - public transportation is less expensive but forces you to conform to the bus's schedule. Renting a car provides the most flexibility but will cost a bit more. With the amount of traveling between destinations we were planning, renting a car made the most sense for us, particularly because the cost would be shared between three people.

Renting a Car

If you choose to rent a car for your Patagonia trip, you have the added benefit of the flexibility of schedule and a place to store items you may not want to carry all of the time, but there will still be some hurdles to climb.

Patagonia encompasses destinations in both Chile and Argentina. A vehicle permit is required to authorize the vehicle to enter and exit each country. Rental car companies have different rules and costs regarding the permit. Some only allow certain classes of vehicles to have this permit, so the cheapest car rental option might not be allowed to cross the border. This information is not clearly stated when you reserve the vehicle online. We, in fact, made a reservation online and learned after booking that we could not indeed cross the border with that car or that car rental company. Even in the fine print, we could not find any restrictions on our initial reservation. Only after we inquired about the permit was this issue revealed to us. You need to request the permit directly from the local rental agency at least seven days prior to arrival to prepare the paperwork. Ultimately, we rented through Avis, but the actual agency in Chile is run by a third-party company called EMS. When you reserve the car through Avis's main reservation site, ask them to give you contact information for the pick-up location so you can call and email yourself to arrange in advance for the permit. The permit is good for as many border crossings as necessary. Getting this right was particularly important since our driving route included several crossings into and out of Argentina from Chile.

Another fact to be aware of is that rental car employees at small airports like Punta Arenas are only present immediately after planes land. Therefore, make sure that you check in to the counter right away and do not dawdle. We learned this the hard way. When we landed we immediately had to deal with a lost baggage issue. By the time we arrived at the car rental counter, the agents were gone, and we subsequently had to wait two hours for the agents to return for the next flight arrival.

Waiting in the Punta Arenas airport for two hours to get rental car

Beware of renting a vehicle from a third-party supplier. For international rentals, stick with making the reservation directly from the rental car company, likely Avis or Europcar. This will ensure that you get accurate information and are dealing with the authorizing agency of your vehicle.

Make sure to read all documentation carefully and bring printed confirmation emails with you! When we arrived, the rental car contract claimed that the permit to cross into Argentina was US$50/day. We provided a copy of an email from their manager stating the permit would cost US$110 for the duration of our trip. They easily made the correction, which brought into question the whole process. That printed out email saved us US$740.

Having a rental car adds to your flexibility but also, influenced our itinerary because it restricted us to start and end at the same location. Dropping off a rental vehicle in a different location causes the price to skyrocket.

Request a diesel vehicle. Diesel is the most economical option in Patagonia, providing the best fuel economy for a low cost. A sedan is an adequate car to navigate the region but try to talk the agents into giving you an upgrade.

Buying fuel in Patagonia is very easy. Each station has attendants who pump the fuel for you and accept payment. All we had to do was stop, ask them for a full tank of diesel and were on our way! One striking note about this region is the lack of any development between the cities. Nothing but grazing sheep and vast landscapes. Be mindful to fill your tank when you have the opportunity because there are no stand-alone gas stations even along the major routes.

Buses

Buses are certainly an option for your Patagonia trip, as we saw them when traveling to each of our destinations. Buses can be the best option for independent travelers, those spending significant time in the region, and if returning to the original destination is not a logical option. Buses are the preferred method of transport for long distance travel. Many companies serve routes from Southern Patagonia to the rest of Patagonia and South America.

Bus-Sur: Punta Arenas, Puerto Natales, Torres del Paine National Park, El Calafate, Ushuaia
Chalten Travel: El Calafate to El Chaltén
Cal-Tur: Los Glaciares National Park, El Chaltén

What Time of Year Should You Visit?

Patagonia is in the southern hemisphere, so the summer months, which are optimal for hiking, are opposite of the northern hemisphere. Determining when to go will be a trade-off between optimal weather and the abundance of fellow travelers. It is simple math:

16

everyone wants to go at the time of year when the weather is best. The tourist season lasts from November-April, January and February are the most popular. Our mid-November start date proved to be a bit early in the season for Torres del Paine as sections in the park were too dangerous to pass. I would suggest arriving in or after December, so the winter has fully passed, and the conditions are optimal for hiking. <u>Wait to book your flight until you have scheduled campsites at Torres del Paine.</u> Flights can be made anywhere from 2-4 months in advance, but if you want to trek through Torres del Paine you need to start the reservation process as soon as sites become available, which is a bit of an uncertainty, but should be around March-April. Advanced planning is unfortunately necessary for this very popular trekking destination.

What Documentation Is Required to Enter Chile and Argentina?

For just about every traveler coming from North America and Europe, there are currently no visa requirements to enter Chile or Argentina. All you need is a valid passport. ** Pro tip: When you pass through the customs in Chile, they will give you an Investigations Police of Chile (PDI) receipt. MAKE SURE TO KEEP THIS WITH YOU!!! Many of the lodging locations required it, and one of the sites charged a harsh penalty for failing to produce it.

What Should I Bring?

This is going to be different to each individual, but here are some general tips and guidelines for equipment you will need:

Do not over pack. More likely than not, you will bring too much "stuff." Every ounce you pack is another ounce you have to carry on your back. Packing is always a process for me. If my pack is full of the items I've selected, I take items out until the bag is only 75-80% full. This always has worked out since I buy things as I go and need the room at the end to bring them back. An exception to this rule is if I am bringing food, as that is space I will gain back throughout the trip.

When traveling with a group, "group gear" is anything that the whole group shares such as cooking supplies, food, tents, and water purification. Make sure that you divide out group gear evenly so that weight is well distributed. Keep this group gear assignment constant throughout the trip so that you always know where to find each item. Before you leave on your trip, have everyone bring their gear to one location, then unpack and repack together. This eliminates unnecessary duplicates and may help you realize that everyone thought someone else was bringing something that no one has actually packed. It is also the best way and time to evenly divide up group gear and food.

Select items in the following equipment list include gear and clothing I recommend based on my own experience with them. Use these as examples, but your own needs will dictate which product is right for you. If you are traveling to Patagonia, you likely have done some hiking before and have much of the equipment listed already. Below is an explanation for those that might not have purchased the necessary items before. For female adventurers, use the items I've provided as a starting point and supplement/exchange as necessary.

Camping Gear

- Backpack. Selecting a pack will be one of the largest and therefore one of the most important investments you make. Having a pack that is the right size for your body and amount of gear you need will severely impact your comfort on the trail. Packs are sized by volume, I recommend the Gregory Baltoro 75L Pack if you plan on going on extended hikes such as the 8-day O-Circuit in Torres del Paine; if not a 65L would be sufficient. When selecting a pack, make sure it has high-quality materials and features, particularly the waist belt padding and compartments that offer easy access to gear when the pack is on your back. Any quality camping store such as REI will be able to help you select the best pack for you.

- Camping Stove. We brought an MSR Dragonfly Stove, which is a bit larger of a unit but gives you the best performance and versatility. If you have an MSR stove, we found white gas, "Becina Blanca," at the hardware store in Puerto Natales. The majority of people we encountered used stoves like Jetboil which use pressurized canisters that are easily found throughout the area. These are great if you are only using the stove to boil water because they are more compact and economical.

- Cookware. Bring cookware that is best suited for the selected stove and what you intend to cook. I love my Light My Fire Mess Kit.

- Sleeping Pad. I used to think that people who use these weren't as rugged as me, but the truth is these are essential only partially because of comfort; their primary purpose is warmth. Having a layer of air in between the ground and your body severely limits the conduction of cold air while you sleep. I use the Thermarest NeoAir.
- Sleeping Bag. If you have a poor-quality sleeping bag, you will regret not upgrading. Patagonia nights are cold even in the summer, one night it snowed on us! Invest in a quality bag that has at least a 20F rating. Sleeping bags come in either synthetic material or down. Down will generally be lighter and more compact but can be difficult to deal with if it gets wet.
- Tent. Although it is possible to rent tents at the various sites in Torres del Paine, it is a good investment to purchase a quality tent. Key features I look for in a standard two-person tent is access (get one with two doors so each person can get in independently) and wind/rain protection. If your group has more than two people, I would recommend having multiple two-person tents instead of purchasing one larger one. 4-person tents are large to the point that they will be too much of a burden on whoever gets stuck carrying it. Bring extra stakes, so you can stake

out the rainfly both perpendicularly and in line with the poles, as well as the corners of your tent (8 total). I've been happy with my REI Half Dome 2 Plus for years now. ** Pro-tip: If you need to distribute weight between members of the group more, have one person carry the tent and the other the poles.

- Water Filtration. Patagonia waters are generally safe to drink without filtration since they come directly from the glacier, but there are some areas where mud accumulates, and horses frequently pass. In Torres del Paine, there is potable running water at many of the sites. You likely won't need to use any treatment but it is good to have a backup. Most water filtration processes involve either chemical or physical separation. I recommend MSR's Autoflow Gravity Filtration Bag, which allows you to filter a large quantity of water with gravity as your source of energy.
- Camelbak Bladder and Nalgene.
- Poop Kit. Yes, everyone poops, especially on the trail. On the trail, follow Leave No Trace principles. This includes burying solid waste in a dug hole 100ft away from the trail and 200ft from a water source. REI sells sanitation trowels that work great and are very

lightweight. Pack a small container of hand sanitizer and toilet paper as well.

- Clothesline. I always bring about 50 feet of thin rope to use as a clothesline knowing it can also help in an emergency situation.

Clothing

The only sure thing about weather in Patagonia is that it is constantly changing. You will be in the far southern hemisphere which means long summer days. In November, the sun rises by 05:30 and sets about 22:00. One hour it will be 70F and sunny, next it's howling wind and rain. Nights are the coldest, reaching down close to 30F depending on the time of year. Layers will allow you to adjust to the various conditions you encounter. It is impressive how different your body feels when you are hiking compared to stagnation. Typical mornings start off with all layers on, but as you start hiking your heart rate goes up and off go the layers. Then stop for any short period of time and the cold wind will tell you to put them back on. The "Game of Layers" will be played throughout your Patagonia journey.

- Rain Gear. This includes a quality rain jacket, rain pants, and a rain cover for your pack. These will be precious pieces of equipment on your trip, make the investment in quality rain gear. Cheaper rain gear loses its water resistance over time! Many packs now come with a rain cover, but purchase separately, if necessary.
- Hiking Boots. Hiking boots are another one of the most important pieces of gear for you on the trail. A good hiking boot will be waterproof and feel stable with a rigid structure that prevents ankle rolls and most importantly must fit you. Wear them on a couple day hikes to see how well they fit your feet and if you feel any hot spots. Salomon's Quest 4D was fantastic.
- 2-3 Synthetic, Non-Cotton T-Shirts
- 1 Lightweight Zip Off Trail Pants. Best ones can be removed with your boots still on!
- 2 Long Sleeve Synthetic Layers
- 1 Thermal Long Underwear
- 1 Down Thermal Layer
- 4-6 Hiking Socks
- 2-3 Hiking Underwear
- Lightweight Synthetic Gloves
- Beanie/Winter Hat

- Site shoes such as Chacos or throw away sneakers. AKA something you can wear when you arrive at a campsite, you'll want to get out of the boots!
- ** Pro-tip: If you are renting a car, you'll have a place to store stuff while you are out hiking. Bring some comfy clothes for car rides that you wouldn't normally take on the trail and maybe even a clean set of clothes for the journey home that you leave in the car throughout the trip.

Miscellaneous Gear

- Travel Documentation
  - Valid Passport. ** Pro-tip: In addition to bringing your passport, bring a photocopy of it, upload a scanned copy to the cloud and to a friend or family member back home. If you lose your passport, it is much easier to get it replaced abroad if you can provide a copy.
  - Printed copies of all reservations including campsites, hostels, rental car, travel insurance, etc.
- Headlamp
- Toiletries (including any medications you might need)
- Pack Towel

- Polarized Sunglasses
- Electrical Adapter-they use Type C plug, same as Europe
- Travel Journal. Great waterproof paper products exist to protect your journal from the elements.
- Multi-tool
- Camera and Camera Tripod
- Duct Tape **Pro-tip: Take a Nalgene and wrap it in layers of duct tape so you don't have to take the whole roll, saves space!
- Padlock for hostels
- Electrical equipment for car (auxiliary cable, cigarette USB charger, phone mount)
- Compactable Daypack
- Camping Pillow – Optional, I typically use clothes bag as a pillow to save space.
- Sleeping Mask
- Playing Cards
- All Purpose Wash Soap
- 2 Carabiners to hang items from pack
- 4 Bandanas – use for cleaning and first aid
- First Aid Supplies. At a minimum, any good trekking first aid kit will include the following:
  - Foot care products: Mole skin, Band-Aids

o Sunscreen. Even when clouds are prevalent, make sure to wear sunscreen as the sun intensity is strong

o Ibuprofen

o Anti-diarrheal. None of us had any issues with food poisoning, but this should be standard for any trip

o Gauze pads

o Athletic tape

o Various size bandages

o Sewing scissors

o Aquaphor or any petroleum jelly product

o Earplugs

Food

Chilean customs allowed all of our packaged food such as freeze-dried dinners, pre-packaged trail mix, energy bars, and beef jerky. Make sure to declare it! They had no problem with any of the food we brought as long as it was sealed and came in a package. There is a grocery store in Puerto Natales where you can purchase other items you may wish for Torres del Paine like fruit, bread, tea, etc.

Smartphone Applications to Download

- Maps.me - This is an absolute must for any traveler. Maps.me provides offline map services with spectacular detail. Google Maps also allows you to download maps for offline usage, but maps.me provides superior detail. When you download the app, download different maps by zooming into a region. I was so impressed to find hiking trails shown on the maps and locations of gas stations, hostels, and restaurants wherever we traveled. Even without cellular data, the GPS in your phone tracks your location. Offline navigation with maps.me puts getting lost in the past.
- Tricount – This application helps keep track of costs for your trip and helps settle who owes what when someone pays for a shared expense.
- WhatsApp – Most of the locals communicate with WhatsApp, an internet-based web communication service.
- TrackMyTour – Allows you to create an online map of your journey for family and friends to follow along. Parents love this as they can see in real time what you are up to and that you are safe.

Trekking Patagonia: A Guide to Your Own Adventure

- MemoTrips – Essentially a digital travel journal, where you can document your journey with pictures and written entries.
- Hostelworld – Popular source to book hostels. Be aware that often prices are cheaper when you inquire directly to the hostel or campsite.
- Booking.com – Many lodging locations in Patagonia use Booking.com. A nice feature about this service is Free Cancellation on most reservations as long as you cancel within a couple days of the reservation.
- TripAdvisor – Get recommendations on activities, lodging, restaurants in each destination.
- Airline App – Keeps track of your boarding passes and on certain flights, you can stream movies and tv shows directly to your device.

Patagonia Travel Map

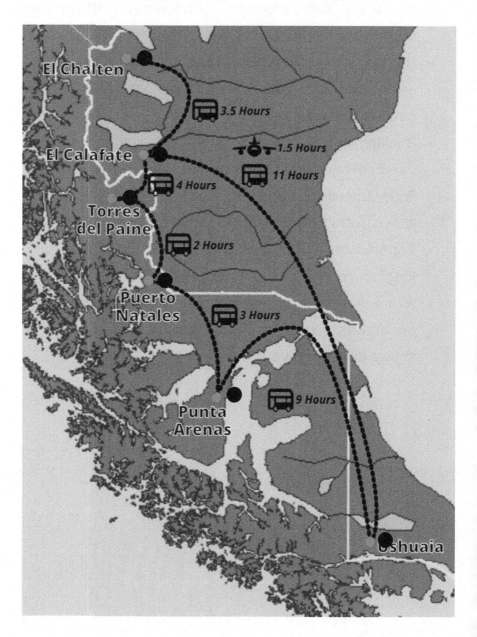

Patagonia Trip Itineraries: For The Trekking Enthusiast

RECOMMENDED: 3-Week Patagonia Itinerary

This itinerary is recommended for any trekking enthusiast looking to experience the highlights of Patagonia.

Days 1-2: Depart home, arrive in Punta Arenas on Day 2. Travel to Puerto Natales from the airport.

Days 3-10: Complete the 8-day O-Circuit at Torres del Paine. Travel to El Calafate the night of Day 10.

Day 11: El Calafate: Perito Moreno Glacier. Travel to El Chaltén.

Days 12-14: El Chaltén: Monte Fitz Roy, Cerro Torre, Loma del Pliegue Tumbado. Add additional rest day if you have time.

Day 15: Travel Day to Ushuaia.

Days 16-19: Ushuaia and Tierra del Fuego National Park. Travel to Punta Arenas.

Days 20-21: Return Home.

** Two days could be eliminated if necessary. Switch from the 8-day to 7-day O-circuit, and eliminate Loma del Pliegue Tumbado from El Chaltén.

2-Week Patagonia Itinerary

Similar to the 3-Week Itinerary, but without the stop in Ushuaia and switching from the O-Circuit to the W-Circuit.

Days 1-2: Depart home, arrive in Punta Arenas on Day 2. Travel to Puerto Natales from the airport.

Days 3-7: Complete the 5-day W-Circuit at Torres del Paine. Travel to El Calafate night of Day 7.

Day 8: El Calafate: Perito Moreno Glacier. Travel to El Chaltén.

Trekking Patagonia: A Guide to Your Own Adventure

Day 9-12: El Chaltén: Monte Fitz Roy, Cerro Torre, Travel to Punta Arenas

Day 13-14: Return Home

10-Day Patagonia Itinerary

Not ideal due to long travel time to hiking time ratio, but is possible if you have very limited time available.

Days 1-2: Depart home, arrive in Punta Arenas on Day 2. Travel to Puerto Natales from the airport.

Days 3-4: 2-Day trip to Torres del Paine National Park

Day 5: El Calafate: Perito Moreno Glacier. Travel to El Chaltén.

Days 6-8: El Chaltén: Monte Fitz Roy, Cerro Torre, Travel to Punta Arenas

Days 9-10: Return Home

Puerto Natales: Gateway to Torres del Paine National Park

Patagonia fjords alongside Puerto Natales

After landing in Punta Arenas, the first stop on your Patagonia adventure will be Puerto Natales, the gateway to Torres del Paine National Park. 99% of travelers in this small town are either arriving from or departing to the park. Since there are no direct bus routes from Punta Arenas to Torres del Paine, Puerto Natales is a necessary stop on your way to the park. Filled with hostels, restaurants, and shops, Puerto Natales is well equipped to prepare you for Torres del Paine. I recommend spending a night here to have an opportunity to talk with other travelers, learn about current trail conditions and acquire any food and equipment you need for the trek. Stay here for only for as long as it will take you to be ready to leave for Torres del Paine.

Getting There

From Punta Arenas, it takes about three hours to travel to Puerto Natales by car or bus. Most flights arrive in Punta Arenas in the early afternoon, allowing you to arrive in Puerto Natales by the evening the same day. The Punta Arenas airport is located 20 minutes north of downtown Punta Arenas, so go straight from the airport to Puerto Natales if you are trying to get to Torres del Paine by the next day. You can enjoy downtown Punta Arenas before you head home. There is frequent bus service from both the airport and downtown Punta Arenas to Puerto Natales with Bus-Sur (8.000 CHP or US$13). If you are driving, the two cities are connected by a single highway, RN 9, making it impossible to get lost. From Torres del Paine, Puerto Natales is two hours away.

Where We Stayed

Vinnhaus, Manuel Bulnes 499, US$20 per night in 10-person dorm

Vinnhaus was a pleasant place to spend our first night in Patagonia. Located right on the main street through the city, it was convenient to walk to nearby shops and restaurants. The 10-person dorm didn't offer privacy but does have impressive bathrooms and showers. The common room is cozy and offers free breakfast. Here we were able to talk amongst fellow travelers and were warned about the treacherous weather-related conditions of the John Gardner Pass. Do not hesitate to reach out and learn about current trail conditions from other travelers. They likely will be your best resource.

Where We Ate

Basecamp, Manuel Baquedano 719, US$10-US$20

Basecamp is attached to the popular Erratic Rock hostel. Their pizza was delicious and offered information on park conditions. Nice environment catered to travelers on the way to Torres del Paine. Modest prices.

Additional City Information

Puerto Natales will be your final chance to purchase gear, food, and supplies for your trip to Torres del Paine. Several outfitters in town can provide anything you may have forgotten. There is a well-stocked grocery store, Unimarc Supermarket, on Manuel Bulnes Street downtown for anything you might need for the trail.

If you have any issues with your reservations in Torres del Paine, the two agencies that operate most of the campsites, Vertice and Fantastico Sur, have offices downtown as well. Remember to fill your car with gas before departing for Torres del Paine!

Next Stop:

Torres del Paine (2 Hours)
Punta Arenas (3 Hours)

Torres del Paine National Park

Without a doubt the crowning jewel of Patagonia, Torres del Paine National Park is an incredible opportunity for avid backpackers to see expansive glaciers, soaring mountains, and breathtaking rock formations. This park is not intended for the novice backpacker. Even sections of trail that cross few topographic lines manage to provide challenging hiking terrain. I call this "Patagonia Flat" hiking. Cold winds, rain, and everything in between force visitors into an incessant battle with nature. But those that can endure the elements are rewarded with profound beauty and wonder that makes it all worth doing.

Getting There

From Puerto Natales

Torres del Paine is located 112km (70 mi) north of Puerto Natales.

By Bus

Check with your hostel in Puerto Natales for the most up to date bus schedules and route information. Buses leave from the Bus Terminal in Puerto Natales at 7:00 AM and 11:30 AM making stops at the Laguna Armaga Terminal and Pudeto Terminal stops (8.000 CHP or US$14). Your end destination will be based on which hiking circuit you choose. If you intend to start hiking at Hotel Las Torres for the "O" Circuit, you will take a bus to Laguna Armaga, then take a second bus to the visitor center (3.000 CHP or US$5). If you plan to start hiking at Refugio Paine Grande for the "W" Circuit, take the same bus but continue to the Pudeto stop where you will hop on the ferry (18.000 CHP or US$30).

By Car

Driving from Puerto Natales to Torres del Paine is straightforward. Navigate to the Laguna Armaga Terminal, where you will pay the park entrance fee. Then proceed to Pudeto Terminal or the Visitors Center. Parking is free both at the Pudeto Terminal if you intend to take the ferry, or by the Visitors Center.

Camping & Refugio Options

Every site at Torres del Paine is operated either by the Chilean governmental agency, CONAF, or two privately owned companies called Vertice and Fantastico Sur. They all have different available amenities and lodging options. Refugios are luxurious accommodations for travelers looking to escape the elements and be treated with a room indoors. Neither tent nor sleeping bag is required. Even though sleeping under a roof is tempting, most hikers opt for the much less expensive camping alternative. Camping sites operated by Vertice and Fantastico Sur provide amenities such as a bathhouse with running water, a shelter where you are permitted to cook meals and escape the weather until around 10:00 PM, and a small shop where you can buy limited overpriced junk food. CONAF's free campsites offer no amenities, just a spot for you to set up a tent. Every site in the park has the Camping option, but only certain locations offer the Refugio option.

Reserving Campsites

As of October 2016, all visitors are required to have reservations. Rangers check throughout various points on the trail to make sure you have a reservation at the location you are in route towards. Reserving campsites in Torres Del Paine is a very difficult logistical process since three different agencies own and operate different campsites and must be contacted individually.

Site	Operator
Hotel Las Torres	Las Torres Patagonia
Refugio Central/Camp Central	FANTASTICO SUR
Camp Seron	FANTASTICO SUR
Refugio/Camp Dickson	VERTICE
Refugio/Camp Los Perros	VERTICE
Camp Paso	CONAF
Refugio/Camp Grey	VERTICE
Refugio/Camp Paine Grande	VERTICE
Camp Italiano	CONAF
Camp Francés	FANTASTICO SUR
Refugio/Camp Los Cuernos	FANTASTICO SUR
Refugio/Camp El Chileno	FANTASTICO SUR
Camp Torres (closed 2018-19)	CONAF

This most challenging part of this trip may not be the hike, but surviving the campground reservation process. Begin this process at least three months in advance of your trip, even more for the January-February months. Arranging an itinerary requires the coordination of campsite availability and reservations with up to three different companies. The 2017-18 season was the first season each of these companies implemented a reservation system. Before then, there were no advanced reservations, so this is progress. Consequently, it will take time to work out the bugs and make the process more seamless. You must remember you are transacting business in a foreign country, one that has a very different definition of promptness and customer service. Only relentless calling and emailing will get results. The communication between the companies and travelers is abysmal. Everyone complains about how impossible it is to book campsites with these companies. You should not expect staff to respond to inquiries for at least three weeks. But don't cancel this part of the trip, the key is perseverance and will absolutely be worth it in the end.

Trekking Patagonia: A Guide to Your Own Adventure

Tips for Reserving Sites:

1. Reserve your campsites before you reserve a plane ticket. This way you can adjust your arrival day based on when you are able to get reservations at the park.
2. Start with CONAF, as these are free sites, and don't result in any loss if you have to change the reservation.
3. Send all correspondences in Spanish. They are much more likely to respond. Either use Google Translate or enlist a kind Spanish-speaking friend to help you.

Costs

Entrance Fee: Foreign Visitors during the High Season (October 1-April 30) is 21,000 CHP, or about US$35, regardless of the duration of stay.

Camping fees are different for every site. Camping at Fantastico Sur and Vertice operated sites cost around US$8-US$12 per person, per night. CONAF operated sites are free. Refugio pricing varies greatly at each location and will be an expensive option for the budget traveler, costing between US$150-US$400 per person, per night.

Vertice and Fantastico Sur offer various services at their locations such as tents, sleeping bags, sleeping pad rentals. Including the camping and equipment fee is in the range of US$30-US$40 per person. Lunch and dinner can be reserved for between US$15-US$25 per person. Even if you are camping, you can reserve meals at the Refugio. It was really nice to pick a night to have a nice prepared cooked meal as a reward for a good day of hiking.

Torres del Paine National Park Trail Map

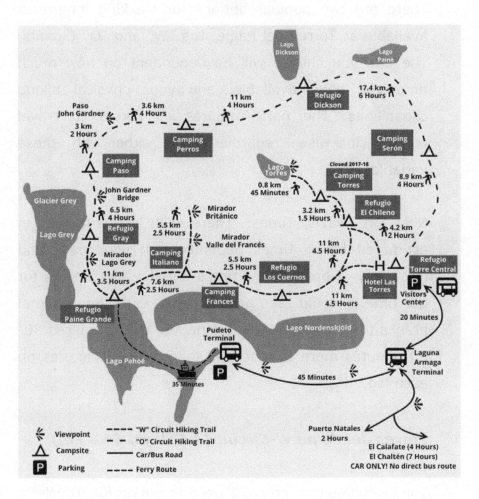

Torres del Paine Hiking Routes and Itinerary

There are two popular options for trekking itineraries available at Torres del Paine, the "W" and "O" Circuits. The one you choose will be dependent on how much time you have available, and your physical hiking capabilities. The park requires all hikers to travel counter-clockwise regardless of either of these variables.

Note on Travel Times: There will be variability in estimated hiking times depending on your pace and frequency of breaks. The times noted are estimates for the time it would take a fit backpacker taking minimal breaks to complete the segment. We often required 30-60 minutes more to stop and take a lot of pictures on each leg.

Torres del Paine W-Circuit (4-5 days, 64.8 km)

The "W" circuit is the most popular option for travelers. Covering about 65 km, or 40 miles, the route includes the iconic highlights of the park, including Glacier Gray, Valle del Francés, and Mirador de Las Torres. The W-circuit will require four to five days depending on pace and time available.

Recommended Itinerary: 5 Day W-Circuit (64.8 km total)

Day 1: Puerto Natales -> Refugio Paine Grande -> Refugio Gray (11 km, 3.5 Hours)

Depart Puerto Natales early in the morning at drive north towards Torres del Paine. Stop at the Laguna Armaga Terminal to pay the park entrance fee. If you are driving, you have two options from here. Option 1: Park at the Pudeto Terminal and hop on the 11:00 AM ferry across Lago Pehoé to Refugio Paine Grande (one way: 18,000CHP or US$30). Option 2: Park at the Visitors Center near Refugio Central, then take two consecutive buses, one back to Laguna Armaga station, then a second to Pudeto. If you choose to park at Pudeto, you will have to take these same buses to get back to your car at the end of the hike. So, it is up to you if you want to deal with this logistical snag before or after the hike. I would recommend contacting Fantastico Sur for details on this bus schedule to get you from the Visitors Center near Refugio Central and

Pudeto Ferry Terminal since it changes throughout the season. This will help you make the decision as well since it may require too early of an arrival at the Visitors Center to get to Pudeto in time for the 11:00 AM ferry, which might not be feasible if you are starting from Puerto Natales. Either way, you'll enjoy the beautiful ferry ride from Pudeto to Refugio Paine Grande. For those taking the bus, you don't have to worry about this. Just take the bus straight from Puerto Natales to Pudeto Ferry Terminal.

Stop and have lunch at Refugio Paine Grande. By 1:00 PM, start your first hike of the trip towards Refugio Gray. Your hike will begin traversing up a beautiful valley with a view of Lago Pehoé over your shoulder. After about an hour, you will arrive at Laguna Los Patos, a small lake with nice lookout points. The remaining hike between Los Patos and Refugio Gray is a good mix of terrain and slope, with beautiful views of Glacier Gray at the Mirador Lago Gray halfway to the end.

View of Lago Gray with Glacier Gray in the distance

You will arrive at Refugio Gray by 4-5PM. Enjoy a nice glass of wine in the cozy Refugio and get ready for the next day!

Day 2: Refugio Gray -> John Gardner Bridge -> Refugio Paine Grande (17.5 km, 6.5 Hours)

Today starts with a beautiful day hike. Leave your tent, grab your daypack, and head northwest on the trail towards Camp Paso. After 45 minutes, you will arrive at the first suspension bridge overlooking the stunning Glacier Gray. Continue another 45 minutes and the John Gardner Bridge gives more amazing photo opportunities.

Approaching Glacier Gray in between Refugio Gray and Camp Paso

Return back to Refugio Gray for lunch and to break camp, then trace your way back to Refugio Paine Grande for the evening.

Day 3: Refugio Paine Grande -> Valle del Francés -> Camp Italiano (18.6 km, 8 Hours)

Get up and depart Refugio Paine Grande by 9:00 AM towards Camp Italiano. After 2.5 hours of "Patagonia Flat" hiking terrain that traces along Lago Pehoé and Lago Skottsberg, you will cross Rio del Francés on a drawbridge and arrive at Camp Italiano. Check in with the ranger, set up camp, and grab your daypack for a hike up the Valle del Francés. It is important to start this hike as soon as possible to ensure you get to the lookouts before the trails close. Italiano to Mirador del Francés lookout closes at 2:00 PM, and from Mirador del Francés to Mirador Británico lookout at 4:00 PM. We never saw these enforced, but be prepared for rangers to stop you if you haven't begun the section before the closing time. An hour of steep hiking up the valley from Camp Italiano will earn you a stunning view from the Mirador del Francés. Many turn back here, but you're in Patagonia to get the most of your adventure, so keep venturing on towards Mirador Británico! After hiking for about another hour, you'll reach a vast rock field that offers fantastic views of the valley and surrounding rock formations. But don't be fooled, this isn't the end. Walk across the field and find the yellow trail marker to find the rest of the trail. Another 30-minute hike with a nice steep section at the end leads to Mirador Británico. Soak in the view, eat a snack, then start the 2.5-hour descent back down to Camp Italiano.

View from Mirador Británico

I recommend staying at Camp Italiano since it is free and you will likely be a bit exhausted at the end of hiking the Valle del Francés, but it does mean the following day will be a bit longer. You could also stay at Los Cuernos that night, shaving a couple miles off the next day, but I suggest saving those miles for the next day which is generally more flat and easier terrain. However, if you plan to stay at Camp Torres the next day, staying at Los Cuernos would be a good idea to better split apart the mileage. Camp Torres was closed for the 2017-2018 season.

Day 4: Camp Italiano -> El Chileno (16.5 km, 7 Hours)

A majority of this hike traces the beautiful Lago Nordenskjöld, with more "Patagonia Flat" terrain.

Lago Nordenskjöld in between Camp Italiano and Refugio Cuernos

Stop for lunch one to two hours after you've passed Los Cuernos as you will be over half way to El Chileno. About two miles after Los Cuernos is a fork in the path, one way leading directly to El Chileno, the other to Hotel Las Torres. Continue towards El Chileno from the fork, where the path winds up a steep ridge and joins with the Valle Ascencio. El Chileno will be along Rio Ascensio. While Camp Torres is closed, El Chileno is the best option to set you up for a sunrise hike up to the Mirador de Las Torres the next day but is expensive. At El Chileno, you are forced to purchase their "platforma premium" option for around US$100 per person, which includes a tent on an elevated platform, sleeping bags, pad, and three meals. We were impressed with the quality of the food we were provided but would have preferred a less expensive option. You can save money by staying at Camp Central down near Hotel Las Torres, but you will have to wake up two hours earlier for the sunrise hike.

Day 5: El Chileno -> Mirador Las Torres -> Puerto Natales/El Calafate (12.2 km, 7 Hours)

Get out of your cozy sleeping bag and leave El Chileno for the Torres at least two hours before scheduled sunrise. Take your time hiking up to the Torres. As with most hiking in Patagonia, while you are moving your body temperature rises, but as soon as you stop your body gets cold from the temperature and wind, especially if your clothes are wet from perspiration.

Trekking Patagonia: A Guide to Your Own Adventure

Take this hike nice and slow to limit perspiration, you will be happy when you get to the top! Bring a sleeping bag to warm up in as you wait for the sun to rise at the summit. If you're lucky, you'll have a clear morning to enjoy the crown jewel of Patagonia.

Sunrise at the Mirador de Las Torres

Only once you've taken ample photographs and soaked in the view for as long as your cold toes can handle, head back down to El Chileno for your hot coffee and breakfast and grab the bag lunch included with your overnight stay. From the Torres, it will take four hours to hike down to Hotel Las Torres. If you parked at Pudeto, you'll have to take the two buses from the

Visitors Center near Refugio Central to Laguna Armaga, then a connecting bus to Pudeto Ferry Terminal. Or you took a bus to Torres del Paine, you can take the 2:00 PM bus from the Visitors Center to Laguna Armaga, then connect to Puerto Natales. If you're driving, you can drive straight from Torres del Paine to El Calafate rather than going back to Puerto Natales. There is no direct bus route from Torres del Paine to El Calafate. You must return back to Puerto Natales even though it is out of the way.

4-Day W-Circuit (64.8 km total)

Similar to the five-day itinerary, but instead of lodging at Refugio Gray, leave your gear upon arrival at Paine Grande, then hike up to Refugio Gray and back. You should arrive back to Paine Grande by 6-7PM. This would likely force you to skip the day hike up to the John Gardner Bridge.

Day 1: Puerto Natales -> Refugio Paine Grande -> Refugio Gray -> Refugio Paine Grande (22 km, 7 hours)

Days 2-4: See 5-Day W Trek Itinerary Starting On Day 3.

Torres del Paine O-Circuit (7-8 Days, 102.8 km)

The O-Circuit of Torres del Paine offers seasoned hikers the opportunity to explore more of the backcountry sections of the park in addition to the main attractions. Less popular relative to the W-Circuit, this hike allows travelers to escape the crowds and see beautiful sections of the park. This trek is a combination of the backcountry sections of the park and the standard W-Circuit. Poor weather conditions on the John Gardner Pass prevented our completion of the entire O-Circuit, however, I will share my recommendations of how to complete the O based on my prior research and communications with fellow travelers there.

Recommended: 8-day O-Circuit Itinerary (102.2 km total)

Day 1: Puerto Natales -> Camp Seron (8.9km, 4 Hours)

Either drive or take the 7:00 AM bus out of Puerto Natales and arrive at the Visitors Center outside the Hotel Las Torres. Finding the trailhead to Camp Seron is a bit tricky. Walk down the road from the Visitors

Center towards Hotel Las Torres, turn right towards the Refugio Torre Central. Keep going past Refugio Torre Central, until you reach an unmarked dirt road on the left side. Follow this road until you reach the trailhead.

Entrance to Seron Sector. Located behind Refugio Central.

From the trailhead, it is about a four-hour hike to Camp Seron. The hike is "Patagonia Flat" with beautiful views of Rio Paine. Beware of horses on the trail, they are often herded right alongside the trail.

Day 2: Camp Seron -> Refugio Dickson (18.5km, 6 Hours)

Similar to Day 1, this is another "Patagonia Flat" hike that first traces along the Rio Paine to the Lago Paine. Lago Dickson is a beautiful spot to set up camp. Make dinner, chat with fellow travelers to learn about current conditions on the John Gardner pass.

Day 3: Refugio Dickson -> Camp Los Perros (11 km, 4 Hours)

Sleep in a bit, this day is a warmup for the next day. From Refugio Dickson to Camp Perros follows the Rio de Los Perros. Get to bed early for an early wake up to begin the ascent up to John Gardner Pass.

Day 4: Refugio Los Perros -> Camp Paso (6.6 km, 6 Hours)

Mid-November proved to be too early in the season to safely ascend the John Gardner Pass. There were a few hikers who reported to us that they made it through, but could not have done it without following a guide as the trail markers were covered in snow and visibility was very poor. Travelers recommend completing this hike as early in the day as possible when the weather is typically best.

Day 5: Camp Paso -> Refugio Paine Grande (17.5 km, 7.5 Hours)

Good news! After a difficult ascent through the John Gardner Pass, this day has a lot of downhill, but still is a good chunk of kilometers to go. Follow Glacier Gray over the two beautiful suspension bridges and eat lunch at Refugio Gray. Continue on to Refugio Paine Grande and arrive by 5:00 PM.

Day 6-8: See 5-Day W-Circuit Days 3-5 for itinerary details.

Note: To make this itinerary seven days, you could go from Dickson to Paso in one day, eliminating the stay at Los Perros. This would be possible but would risk starting the pass later in the day. The pass from Los Perros to Paso closes at 3:00 PM. The operating companies will not allow you to make reservations for segments they believe are too aggressive to accomplish in a single day, such as from Seron to Perros, or from Perros to Paine Grande.

Park Rules

No open fires or drones are allowed inside the park. Stoves are allowed, but only in designated locations at the campsites.

Miscellaneous Torres del Paine Tips

- The road from Laguna Armaga to Pudeto is stunning and provides some amazing lookouts of the park. Especially if you are driving, allow an hour to drive through that section of the park and stop at the lookout spots for some great photo ops. You will do this anyway if you follow the W itinerary, but those following the O itinerary might accidentally miss this.

- Kayaking tours are available from Refugio Gray onto Lago Gray. We met a group that fit this half-day tour into their schedule and greatly enjoyed it.
- Trails are well marked throughout the park; only finding the Seron trail from the Visitors Center at Las Torres proved difficult.

Next Stop

El Calafate (4 Hours, CAR ONLY)
Puerto Natales (2 Hours)

El Calafate: Gateway to Los Glaciares National Park

After you've finished exploring the wonder of Torres del Paine National Park, head to El Calafate, the gateway to Los Glaciares National Park. With the expansive Perito Moreno Glacier, El Calafate will be a bit of a break from the ruggedness of Torres del Paine and offers you a chance to have a nice dinner and do some shopping. La Anonima is a great local grocery store to stock up on supplies. A variety of banks on the Avenida del Liberator General San Martin have ATMs where you should withdraw enough cash to last you for your time in El Calafate and El Chaltén since El Chaltén does not have any ATMs. Only one day is needed to get the most out of El Calafate and the neighboring Perito Moreno Glacier.

Getting There

By Car

If you are driving, it takes about four hours to drive to El Calafate directly from Torres del Paine. From the Laguna Armaga Terminal, drive towards Cerro Castillo.

There is a border control station on 251-CH right after you pass through the roundabout. Enter the border control building for authorization to exit Chile. None of the border control stops are clearly marked nor have instructions telling you what to do. At each of the border control stations, there is a counter that first handles the customs for each individual, then another counter to authorize the vehicle entering and leaving the country. When entering a new country, they will ask you to declare any plant/animal products. We did not have any problem with our trail mix, but apples and honey were confiscated. After entering Argentina, head north on RN 40. There will be a route sign to turn left on RP 7 towards El Calafate, but DO NOT TAKE IT! This road includes a very long stretch of dirt and gravel road that risks getting a flat tire. It might be the most direct route, but do not put yourself and your car through that misery. Continue the long way along RN 40 through Esperanza, then north up to El Calafate.

By Bus

By bus, you will come from Puerto Natales, not Torres del Paine. This route is very popular and should be booked in advance. Bus-sur offers departures from

Puerto Natales at 7:15 AM, 7:30 AM, and 2:30 PM. The bus costs 20.000 CHP, or US$33.

Where We Stayed

El Ovejero, José Pantin 64, US$8-US$12

My goal when traveling is to allocate as small a portion of my budget towards lodging as possible. I would rather spend money on food, activities, and unexpected expenses. We thus chose to stay at El Ovejero, a campground right near the main street of downtown since it is inexpensive but still provides sufficient amenities. El Ovejero offers campsites and dormitories for about the same price. No advanced reservation was required. Tours to Perito Moreno Glacier and El Chaltén can be organized with the front desk.

Where We Ate

Wanaco Tradicional Bar, Av. del Libertador Gral. San Martín 1091, US$15-US$25

Wanaco is a great place to go if you are looking to grab a drink and enjoy some pub food. A large menu provides various options like lamb burgers, salads, sandwiches, and other items that will be a welcome change from the freeze-dried trail food. Stay away from the Bloody Mary.

Pietro's Café, Av. del Libertador Gral. San Martín 1002, US$15-US$25

Pietro's Café was one of the few options we could find open in the morning for breakfast. Enjoy some delicious waffles for breakfast, or sandwiches, empanadas, and pizza for lunch or dinner.

Banana waffle at Pietro's Café

Doña Mecha, Cmte. Tomás Espora 35, US$8-US$12

Before driving to El Chaltén, we stopped at Doña Mecha to pick up a dozen empanadas. They also have a variety of pizzas and sandwiches. Delicious, and well-priced, but did require a 20-minute wait. Place your order, then go browse the neighboring shops until it is ready.

Los Glaciares National Park: Glaciar Perito Moreno

Glaciar Perito Moreno in Los Glaciares National Park

From El Calafate, it is about an hour drive west along RP 11 to the Perito Moreno Glacier. Local companies offer roundtrip bus rides to and from the glacier. If you take the bus, sit on the left side for best views! As you enter the park, you will pay a US$30 per person entrance fee. This impressive glacier is popular for tourists to visit since you can easily drive right up and walk to the viewing platforms. When you get to the glacier entrance, a ranger will direct you to the main parking lot. From there you take a free five-minute shuttle to the viewing platforms. Take a walk all around the different platforms for a good view. As you walk, that BOOM sound isn't thunder, but large chunks of the glacier falling off. Keep your eye out, you might get lucky and see it for yourself.

El Chaltén: The Trekking Capital of Patagonia

El Chaltén is pure paradise for the backpacking and trekking junky. With a large network of trails, El Chaltén provides access to the northern section of Los Glaciares National Park including the iconic Monte Fitz Roy and mesmerizing Cerro Torre. The city of El Chaltén is a small town at the base of the valley and has a true backpacker vibe. Everyone visiting El Chaltén has a pack on and is there for some amazing hiking. An abundance of restaurants and lodging options offer a fantastic complement to the wide breadth of trekking activities available.

A minimum of two full days are required to enjoy the highlights of the park, but you could easily be entertained in El Chaltén for a week. If you have flexibility in your schedule, allow an extra day than you predict to use as either a rest day or in the likely event of inclement weather. Unlike trekking in Torres del Paine, each hike can be accomplished in a day, allowing you to go off for a hike and return to town for a great meal and a comfortable stay. For those looking to camp within the park, there are options for that as well. No entrance fee or reservations are required for the trails and campsites. The weather in El Chaltén follows the same pattern as the rest of Patagonia: completely unpredictable. Local grocery stores are available to stock up on trail food for your trek, but you will not find an ATM.

Getting There

From El Calafate, El Chaltén can easily be reached by car or bus and will take about 2.5 hours. Chaltén Travel offers bus service from El Calafate to El Chaltén at 8:00 AM, 1:00 PM, and 6:00 PM for about US$35. Roads are pleasantly paved, but with no services whatsoever in between, so make sure to fill up on gas before departing. Fantastic views of Monte Fitz Roy and Cerro Torre will greet you as you approach.

Monte Fitz Roy along the drive into El Chaltén

El Chaltén can also be reached from the north with connecting bus services from Bariloche.

Where We Stayed

El Relincho, San Martín 219, US$8-US$12

In El Chaltén, there is no shortage of hostels filled with backpackers getting ready to go on a hike the next day. Most hostels in town cost between US$20-US$30 per person. We opted for the cheaper camping option at El Relincho. Located on the main street of El Chaltén, it provides walking access to the main trails to Monte Fitz Roy and Cerro Torre, as well as neighboring restaurants. They also offer limited inexpensive dorms. We greatly enjoyed our experience at El Relincho, no prior reservation was required for camping. There is a building with a cozy common area and access to a kitchen as well as sufficient bathrooms with ample hot water for a nice shower.

Where We Ate

Trekking Patagonia: A Guide to Your Own Adventure

Patagonicus, Andreas Madsen 11, US$12-US$20

Our first dinner in El Chaltén was a fantastic greeting to the city. Their pizzas with lamb and a variety of cheeses are delicious. Patagonicus has a very warm atmosphere with wooden booths and no lack of food and drink options for the hungry hiker.

La Vineria, Lago del Desierto 265, US$15-US$25 per person

After a long hike, a stop at the Wine Bar, La Vineria, was a perfect way to end the day. The small, intimate environment of La Vineria offers travelers a great place to recover from the long hike of the day. Offering delicious food to accompany the abundance of wine options, you can't go wrong at La Vineria. Cheese platters, empanadas, and pizzas are their specialty. Bring a deck of cards and enjoy this great establishment.

Che Empanada, San Martin 535, US$2-US$8 per person

Che Empanada is a delicious fast food empanada place and is very convenient if you want to bring a snack with you on the trail or in the car on your way out of the city. With a wide variety of empanadas, this reasonably priced location will satisfy your empanada craving.

Heladería Domo Blanco, San Martín 164, US$5-US$8

Reward yourself after a long hike with a stop at this incredible ice cream shop. Quite possibly the best ice cream I have ever had. Offering a plethora of flavors, everyone can get what they want. Prices are a bit on the expensive side, but it was totally worth it. Highly recommended!

El Chaltén Park Map

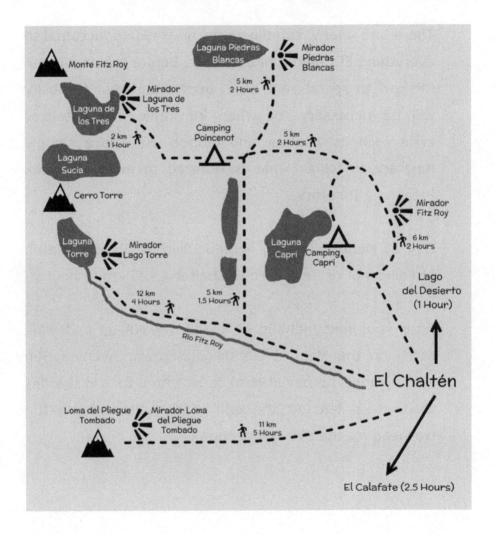

El Chaltén Trekking Itinerary

There are many combinations of ways to accomplish everything El Chaltén has to offer. Before making a plan for how to spend your time, understand that flexibility will be necessary for when inevitable circumstances arise such as weather and fatigue. Here is a sample itinerary to follow what is referred to in the 3-Week Patagonia Itinerary.

Day 1: Monte Fitz Roy, Mirador Piedras Blancas, Camp at Poincenot or Return To El Chaltén (~25 km, 9 hours)

After your first night in El Chaltén, wake up and walk north on the Main street through town, Avenida San Martin, until the paved road turns into a fork in the dirt road. Keep left. At the end of the dirt road is the trailhead for the Fitz Roy section.

Monte Fitz Roy trailhead sign in El Chaltén

The first 90 minutes of hiking is very uphill and provides stunning views of the Rio de Las Vueltas. Soon after, a fork in the road will direct you towards Laguna Capri or Mirador Fitz Roy. Take the right towards Mirador Fitz Roy, which you will reach within 30 minutes. Another two hours of hiking along the Chorillo del Salto river will bring you to another fork, follow the signs towards Camp Poincenot. Soon after, another fork splits the trail towards the Piedras Blancas and Poincenot. Continue to Camp Poincenot, which is just another half kilometer away. Set up camp, eat some lunch, then grab your daypack (make sure to bring your rain gear!) and begin the ascent up to the Lago de Los Tres at the base of

Monte Fitz Roy. Note throughout the hike, signs do not direct you to Monte Fitz Roy, but to the Lago de Los Tres. From Camp Poincenot, the hike up to Lago de Los Tres is a strenuous hour-long hike with substantial altitude gain.

Monte Fitz Roy behind the Laguna de Los Tres

After enjoying the view of Monte Fitz Roy, make sure to walk around the Laguna de Los Tres on the left side until you reach the viewpoint of Laguna Sucia.

Laguna Sucia from the lookout point adjacent to Laguna de Los Tres

Descend back to Camp Poincenot, and if you have a couple more hours of hiking left in you, follow the sign you passed earlier towards the Mirador Piedras Blancas. Incoming inclement weather prevented us from doing this section but it was highly recommended by fellow travelers.

If you prefer to return to El Chaltén for the night, the hike to Monte Fitz Roy and back to El Chaltén is definitely possible in a single day.

Day 2: Cerro Torre (19km, 6 Hours)

From Camp Poincenot, it is only a two-hour hike to the base of the Cerro Torre, follow signs for the Laguna Torre.

Base of Cerro Torre in front of Laguna Torre

Spend some quality time taking in the view before you begin the three to four-hour descent back into El Chaltén. The hike from Cerro Torre to El Chaltén is very straightforward, with less gradient relative to the Fitz Roy hike.

If you opted to go back to El Chaltén from Monte Fitz Roy, the trail up to Cerro Torre can be found by taking Los Huemules west off of Avenida San Martin. Follow the road uphill. The hike will be 24km.

Find this sign along Avenida San Martin. Follow up to Cerro Torre trailhead.

Day 3: Loma del Pliegue Tumbado (22km, 9 hours)

This hike covers much more ground and altitude gain compared to the milder hikes to Fitz Roy and Cerro Torre, but you are rewarded with impeccable views of both Fitz Roy and Cerro Torre from the top. The trail is found on the south side of the city, on the other side of Rio Fitz Roy. Be ready for physical fatigue to become a factor at this point in the trip. Your group may or may not have the stamina to complete this hike directly after completing the Monte Fitz Roy and Cerro Torre treks. Be smart and make a decision that best fits the needs of the group. If your schedule permits, plan on taking a rest day before attempting this hike or complete it first on fresher legs.

Additional El Chaltén Tips

- Again, make sure you already have cash before coming to El Chaltén. We did not find any ATMs.
- There is a single gas station in town, but it should not be relied upon. Getting gas in El Calafate is the safer option.

Next Stop

El Calafate (2.5 Hours)

Ushuaia (15 Hours by Car, or fly through El Calafate)

Torres del Paine (6 Hours)

Puerto Natales (6 Hours)

Punta Arenas (8.5 Hours)

Ushuaia and Tierra del Fuego: The End of the World

Tierra del Fuego National Park, near Laguna Esmeralda

Ushuaia and Tierra del Fuego National Park is as far south as south goes, not counting Antarctica. This region of Patagonia offers a new type of terrain and glaciers to explore, as well as a variety of boat tours for travelers wishing to get a glimpse of some penguins. During our time in Ushuaia, we focused on hiking and found some unbelievable sites etched with turquoise waters, expansive valleys, and towering mountains that will satisfy the explorer in you. Many travelers who come to Ushuaia use it primarily as a launch pad for trips to Antarctica and miss out on the beauty that Tierra del Fuego National Park has to offer. Trips to Antarctica are expensive, but we met several travelers that found ways to embark on the journey on a science vessel to save on cost. If you have at least a week and ample funds, the trip would definitely be worth looking into. Ushuaia was certainly the most expensive place we visited, with hostels costing over US$30 per person, and meals consistently in the US$20-US$30 range. However, a budget traveler can find options to save on food and lodging by staying away from the expensive tours offered by local companies. Although the terrain does not offer the same jaw-dropping rock formations found in Torres del Paine and El Chaltén, you will find a different sort of beauty in the forests and lakes surrounded by a mountain range capped in snow. Trails here are in general difficult to find without any insider tips.

Getting There

By Plane

If you did not rent a car, the easiest way to access Ushuaia is by plane. Travel by bus to the El Calafate airport. The 90-minute plane ride from El Calafate will be preferable to many travelers compared to the 13 hours on the road. Aerolineas Argentina offers direct flights from El Calafate to Ushuaia for US$150-US$250 one way. Without a car, you can easily travel to all of the locations listed with a cab.

By Bus

This is not recommended. By bus, you would have to go from El Calafate to Puerto Natales to Punta Arenas to Ushuaia. By the time you pay for three buses it almost will equal the plane fare and takes too much time.

By Car

From El Chaltén, the commute includes 13 hours of driving, several border crossings and a car ferry. The total commute will take approximately 14 hours. We opted to complete the journey from El Chaltén by car in one day. For some this would not be feasible, so split up the drive by stopping in Rio Gallegos for a night. South of Rio Gallegos is the first border crossing at Monte Aymond. Border crossings are not clearly marked, and instructions are not direct. Keep an eye on your maps.me as it marks the different border control buildings. In the same building at Monte Aymond, we exited Argentina and entered Chile. Chile was stricter with plant and animal products brought in the country. Continue south on 255-CH past Punta Delgada then turn left on 257-CH towards Ushuaia. Soon after, you will reach the Punta Delgada ferry that will take you and your vehicle across the channel.

Punta Delgada ferry towards Ushuaia

This ferry consistently runs from 8:30AM-1AM and leaves every 20 minutes. Upon boarding the ferry, walk into the cabin to pay the vehicle fee (15,000 CHP, $500 ARG, or US$35). Continue on 257-CH to San Sebastián border control station where you exit Chile and enter Argentina. Stop in Rio Grande to fill up on gas. It is about 3 more hours more down to Ushuaia. As you approach Ushuaia there will be a police checkpoint where they check for a driver's license.

Where We Stayed

Camp Kelenkeskes, Camino del Valle, US$12

Camp Kelenkeskes

As previously mentioned, Ushuaia is tough to travel on a budget. Camp Kelenkeskes proved to be a phenomenal choice for our stay in Ushuaia for its affordability and the helpfulness of its owner, Mauro. The camp is on Mauro's family property, where he lives with his children. Mauro proved to be an invaluable resource and was extremely kind. His property is a bit hard to find, but turn north on Camino del Valle from RN 3, then take a slight left up the road uphill, and his property will be on the right side. Mauro can be contacted through the campsite's Facebook Page. The amenities are basic, including a small shelter and portable bathroom/shower. But the fire pit proved to be a really nice feature as it was the only time we had a campfire in our entire time in Patagonia. When we arrived, Mauro helped us develop a plan and even picked us up from the end of the hike in Tierra del Fuego back to our car. Highly recommended!!!

Where We Ate

Food will be more expensive in Ushuaia compared to the other locations in Patagonia. There were many options in the downtown area, so make sure to do some of your own research before you go. Here is a review of the places we went to. Note that restaurants typically were not open until 7:30 PM.

Estancia Parilla, Gdor, Pedro Godoy 155, US$25-US$35

Estancia Parilla was pricey, but the all you can eat buffet of lamb, sausage, beef, salad, empanadas, and much more was not only delicious but a really fun experience. They have many options for desserts including the delicious apple pie with vanilla ice cream. There are a few other all-you-can-eat BBQ places in town for a little less money, but Estancia Parilla is worth the extra five dollars for the quality of the food.

Dublin – Irish Pub, 9 de Julio 168, US$15-US$25 per person

I would only recommend this Irish Pub if you are looking for a place to grab a drink after dinner or a day of hiking, not for the food. The steak and burger were far below Western standards. But the environment was much more suited for a bar anyway. Not the place to go if you're looking to get local cuisine.

Ushuaia and Tierra del Fuego National Park Map

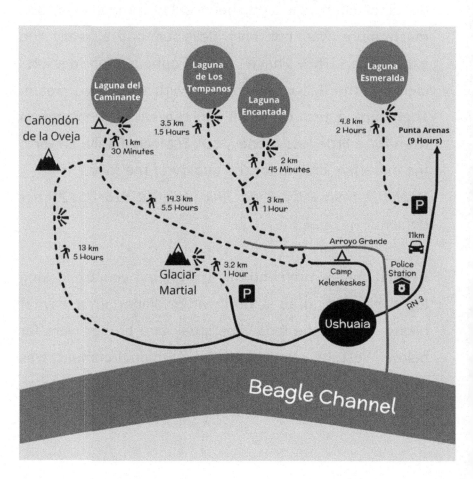

Ushuaia and Tierra del Fuego National Park Itinerary

Thanks to Mauro from Camp Kelenkeskes, we were able to take full advantage of our time in Ushuaia. Each day included rewarding hikes through thick mud and terrain to arrive at a beautiful destination. This itinerary is for those trying to travel this area independently and get a lot of hiking accomplished in a small amount of time. Add an extra day if you are interested in taking a boat tour of the Beagle Chanel!

Day 1: Glaciar Martial and Laguna Esmeralda Day Hikes (16km, 6 Hours)

On your first day in Ushuaia, begin with these two relatively easy day hikes: first to the Glaciar Martial, and second to the Laguna Esmeralda.

The 20-30 minute drive to the base of Glaciar Martial is easy from downtown Ushuaia. Park your car at the base of the Glaciar, and start your initial hike up the large dirt path. It is very wide because in the winter it acts as a ski run! Look to your right and you'll see the chairlift that operates during ski season. After the twenty minutes to the top of the chairlift, continue up the marked path along the river for another 30 minutes all the way to the top lookout point.

Summit of Glaciar Martial

This was our first experience hiking in the snow! Patches of the trail forced you to trek across about a foot deep of snow. Enjoy the view from the top, then head back to the car by lunchtime. You could head into town for a quick lunch before continuing to Laguna Esmeralda.

Drive back through downtown along RN 3 and pass the police station as you exit the city heading east. Another 11 km and you will see a dirt rest stop on the left side, park your car there and enter the Laguna Esmeralda trailhead on the south side of the stop. This trail was our first encounter with the extremely muddy conditions that Tierra del Fuego had to offer. Make sure you have good waterproof boots that won't come off your feet in the mud! Hiking up to the Laguna takes about two hours, and after traversing over muddy trail you are rewarded with a beautiful view of the Laguna Esmeralda. Drive back into town and reward yourself with a nice dinner before returning to Camp Kelenkeskes.

Laguna Esmeralda

Day 2: Laguna de Los Tempanos and Laguna Encantanda Day Hikes (11km, 6.5 Hours)

The beginning part of this hike is difficult to find since there are barely any trail markers until you are over a mile in. From Camp Kelenkeskes, drive west on the same road until you reach the gate shown below:

Entrance gate at the end of Camino del Valle road

Park your car here. The gate is locked for vehicles, but the pedestrian gate on the right side opens. Continue walking along the two-track dirt road for five minutes, then turn left here:

Path towards Laguna de Los Tempanos after entrance gate

Walk along this two track for 10 minutes until you reach a sign directing you towards either the Laguna de Los Tempanos or Laguna Caminante. Turn right towards Laguna de Los Tempanos. Walk through the field until you reach the river. Follow the river west until you find the bridge to cross the river and start the trail.

Bridge to cross over Arroyo Grande towards Laguna de Los Tempanos

When you cross the bridge, the trail becomes well defined for most of the way. Keep your eye out for little yellow and blue trail markers on trees marking the trail. Hike first up to Laguna de Los Tempanos, as it is the more impressive of the two, and you may decide after that hike that you do not have the energy to continue to Laguna Encantada. From the bridge, it is about two hours up to the Laguna de Los Tempanos, through very muddy terrain and good steady incline with switchbacks. More impressive than Laguna Esmeralda, Laguna de Los Tempanos is a beautiful turquoise lake surrounded by snowy mountains. Hike to the other side of the lake on the right side to find an ice cave to explore!

Laguna de Los Tempanos

Hike back down the trail, and if you have time and energy, hike up to the Laguna Encantada for views of another beautiful landscape. The total hike will take you about 6 hours, but with exploring around Laguna de Los Tempanos, and getting a little lost, the whole day took closer to 8 hours for us.

After dinner down in Ushuaia, find the iconic "El Fin Del Mundo" sign along the Beagle Channel. Here you can prove that you were in the southernmost city in the world. There's a parking lot across from Gobernador Godoy road by the lake where you will find the sign.

Great photo to mark your journey to the end of the world. Return back to Camp Kelenkeskes for a bonfire!

El Fin del Mundo: Ushuaia, Argentina

Day 3: Tierra del Fuego National Park to Laguna Caminante (15.3 km, 6 Hours)

Today is not a day hike, you will need to check out of Camp Kelenkeskes and grab all your gear and food for an overnight trek. Start the day early and return to the same gate as yesterday, but this time when you reach the sign, take a left towards Laguna Caminante. The trail from there runs through the forest that lines the valley. Keep your eye out for horses that graze around here. After about 4-5 hours of hiking, the trail will become very steep until you reach the upper edge of the forest that opens to an incredible view of the surrounding valley.

Follow the sign to Laguna Caminante. From here to the Laguna is some of the best stretches of trail I have ever hiked on. Without another soul anywhere around you, the unbelievable views of the expansive natural park can be seen for as far as you can see. Be careful along this section, as the trail traces along the slope of the mountainside.

Views of Tierra del Fuego near Laguna Caminante

After 30 minutes you will reach the beautiful Laguna Caminante. Set up camp in the designated camping area and enjoy what was our favorite campsite of the entire trip. Being completely alone at this gem was a true highlight of our trip. After setting up camp, walk around the lake to the other side and enjoy an unforgettable view of the laguna and the surrounding mountains. Enjoy the waterfall that enters the laguna, and keep your eye out for otters in the water! Dinner tonight can be something more elaborate, try making some pasta with local sausage bought at the local grocery store or your own favorite non-freeze dried trail dinner. Go to bed early to get ready for a big day to come.

Laguna Caminante in Tierra del Fuego National Park

Day 4: Cañondón de la Oveja, Drive to Punta Arenas

Wake up before 7:00 AM and be on the trail by 8:00 AM. Head back along the trail and follow the signs for the Cañondón de la Oveja. This pass through the mountains is a steady uphill battle along rock and snow. You will reach the summit in about two hours.

Cañondón de la Oveja in Tierra del Fuego National Park

After enjoying the view, continue on all the way to where the trail meets Ushuaia. This hike has spots through snow that, unless you have tracks to follow, can be difficult to trace. Keep looking for yellow wooden stakes marking the trail along the path.

After about 3 hours of descent, you will weave through some farmland until reaching RN 3. If you stayed at the Camp Kelenkeskes, arrange a pick-up with Mauro along RN 3 around 2:00 PM. He will drive you back to the campsite where you left your vehicle. If not, you could hitchhike the 15-minute drive back into downtown Ushuaia.

If you are following the 3-Week itinerary, it requires you to make the 9-hour drive up to Punta Arenas upon your return to Ushuaia. This was a grind for us but totally doable. We arrived at our hostel in Punta Arenas by 11:00 PM. If you have an extra day, stay in Ushuaia for one more night and depart for Punta Arenas the following morning. The drive to Punta Arenas is straightforward, and by now you will be a pro at getting through the border crossings.

Next Stop

Punta Arenas (9 Hours)

Punta Arenas: Gateway to Patagonia

Punta Arenas is the gateway to Patagonia. With frequent flights from Santiago, this will likely be your hub in and out of Patagonia. Of all the cities mentioned in this guide, Punta Arenas was the largest and most urban. A large variety of restaurants and lodging options are available downtown. Downtown Punta Arenas is located about 20 minutes south of the Carlos Ibáñez del Campo International Airport. Right along the Strait of Magellan, you will have one last opportunity to do some souvenir shopping before departing back home. The vibrant city is the only place without an emphasis on trekking, but more so on typical lives of the locals. Seeing the local children go to school, prepare to attend a wedding, and go to work were fun ways to experience a bit of the culture while in Patagonia.

Where We Stayed

Samarce House, Av. España 940, US$20-US$25

The Samarce House in Punta Arenas was an excellent final lodging option for our trip. After weeks on the trail, it was with open arms that we accepted a good night sleep in a real bed. The physical building is a family home, with six rooms on the lower level available for travelers. The owner was very friendly and accommodating to us when we informed him about our late check in. Breakfast of eggs and toast was included and prepared for us in the morning. The only downside was the single bathroom for use among the entire hostel. We got a three-person room for about US$70.

Where We Ate

La Chocolatta, Gobernador Carlos Bories 852, US$6-US$20

La Chocolatta is on one of the main tourist streets in Punta Arenas and features a warm atmosphere perfect for grabbing a hot drink and enjoying a game of cards. They had the best hot chocolate I have ever had. Real thick whip cream that most definitely did not come from a can. It is on the pricey side, about US$6 a drink, but make them last and stay awhile to get your money's worth. You can also get great sandwiches and other lunch items.

Empanadas Don Lazaro, Avenida Republica 202, US$7-US$10

The best empanadas of our entire trip were found at Empanadas don Lazaro. A dozen of their delicious beef and cheese empanadas to share satisfied our need to get one last batch of empanadas before hopping on a plane home.

Patagonia Trip Costs

19 Day Patagonia Trip Cost ($USD/Person, 3 People Total)		
Food	$	364
Camping and Hostel Fees	$	340
Flight	$	1,383
Rental Car	$	272
Gas	$	71
Park Entrance Fees	$	66
Miscellaneous (Souvenirs, etc.)	$	130
Travelers Insurance	$	99
TOTAL TRIP COST	**$**	**2,726**

The total cost for our Patagonia Trip was about US$2,750 per person, or an average of US$143/day per person. It is a hefty price tag but compared to the US$7,000+ cost for professionally organized trips that cover less territory in less time, we were pretty happy with how far we were able to stretch every dollar. This tour price doesn't even include airfare! However, these guided trips can definitely be worth it to the right traveler. They offer knowledgeable guides, gear rental, and most of all they take care of all the planning. I always strive to travel independently to gain the freedom and flexibility of setting my own schedule, and to stay within a manageable budget. I believe anyone can successfully navigate Patagonia independently without a professional guide service.

The roundtrip flight was the most significant cost. Since transportation costs will likely be the largest incurred trip expense, the more time you spend in one place, your per-day cost will decrease. This cost estimate does not include any purchased gear. If you are a new backpacker without your own inventory of gear, estimate another US$500-US$1,000 of investment. But then you will have all that gear for your next trip!

International Travel Tips and Tricks

Flying Internationally

Congratulations! You are embarking on an international journey to Patagonia. Flying internationally is much more involved than domestic, with more obstacles and considerations. Here are a few lessons integral to successfully making it to your final destination.

- Checked baggage needs to be picked up and processed through customs as soon as you enter your destination country, not necessarily your destination city. For example, our flight to Punta Arenas from the US went through Santiago. We had to pick up our baggage at baggage claim in Santiago, process it through customs, then recheck the bag for our final flight to Punta Arenas. You'll be disappointed if you assumed your bags will be waiting for you in Punta Arenas and learn they are sitting in Santiago. In some countries, there is a designated recheck-in location for this, but in Chile, you have to go through the whole check in process again for the final leg.
- Do not strap items such as tents and hiking poles to the outside of your pack and expect them to be there

when you pick them up. Even if they are securely attached, it will not stop a thief. Many airlines will wrap your pack in plastic to protect the straps and keep the bag clean upon request. Ask for an extra bag to carry with you for the trip back home.

- Customs will stamp your passport and give you some form of a receipt. Make sure to keep the receipt with you for the duration of your trip. Many countries will want the receipt upon your departure from the country, and lodging often requires it upon check in.

- Do not trust that a generated flight itinerary will provide you with sufficient layover time. At least a 90-minute layover is recommended for all international segments, particularly when you are entering your destination country since you need extra time to get through customs. Travel sites will generate an itinerary that theoretically will work but might force you to sprint through the airport to make the next leg. And that's if everything goes right beforehand.

- Make sure that your passport is not only valid upon your departure and return, but for an extended period after your scheduled return. Different countries have different regulations on how long your passport must be valid beyond the dates of your trip, usually around 3 months.

Cash or Credit? How to Handle $$ Internationally

Traveling in another country with foreign currency is a game with many moving parts. Think of foreign currency as another good that you are buying for the trip. When you use an ATM, you are paying the local bank a certain amount of your local currency for the foreign currency. The "price" of this foreign currency is based on current exchange rates as well as transaction fees assigned by both the foreign bank to give you foreign currency and your home bank to convert its currency to the foreign bank. Just like picking a hotel, if you are getting the same product, in this case, a fixed amount of foreign currency, you want to buy it at the lowest price.

In most Asian countries, a majority of financial transactions are made in cash, while other countries have greater ability to process credit cards. Knowing the policies and fees on your credit cards and ATMs will dictate the best way for you to spend money. Travel credit cards with your preferred airline are a great way to accumulate rewards for travel and to save on foreign transaction fees. In general, if you can use a travel credit card with no fee, do it. The credit card likely has a better conversion rate compared to what you will get from a foreign bank's ATM.

However, not every merchant will accept credit cards and will require local currency. ATM withdrawals can quickly become a large expense with no reward. Typically, the foreign bank and your home bank will both charge you a flat fee for every withdrawal. Research options with local credit unions that offer a small percentage fee for each withdrawal instead of a flat rate. That way, there is no inhibitor to making multiple withdrawals throughout the trip.

When withdrawing from an ATM, there is a balance between taking too much and too little cash out. Take out too little cash, and you will have to withdraw again and possibly incur another fee. Take out too much, and you are at greater risk of having your money lost or stolen. The goal is for you to not be left with any foreign currency upon departure. Currency exchange companies are notoriously cheap and will offer far less for the same money as you paid for it. If you are left with cash, avoid currency exchanges at the airport and try to exchange cash at local banks in the city. For any credit or debit card you plan on using internationally, make sure to alert your bank in advance to prevent the unwanted closure of your account.

In Patagonia, credit cards are widely accepted at restaurants, lodging, and gas stations. Even the campsites inside Torres del Paine accepted credit cards. Try to use your credit card as much as possible. If it does not have foreign transaction fees, you will get the best conversion rate. Sometimes merchants require a minimum balance in order to use the credit card. Cash will still be needed for other purchases.

International Phone Service

Depending on your phone carrier, there will be different options for international phone service. Most plans now have two options: a cheaper option that is a flat monthly fee with unlimited texting and a very small data package, or a higher daily fee to keep your same plan as you have at home. I recommend the cheaper option and just stick to Wifi for all of your data needs. After all, you're here to experience nature, not

Facebook right? Make sure that data consuming applications are switched off of data in your phone settings, as well as iMessage for iPhone users.

Traveler's Insurance

Traveler's insurance provides protection for different risks associated with the trip, mainly personal health and financial. Plans and coverages vary greatly by the provider. The first reason to get traveler's insurance is that most health insurances do not cover international travel. If you get hurt in a remote area and have to go to the hospital, you could be responsible for some major medical bills. Make sure to get a plan that has substantial medical coverage. The second reason to purchase traveler's insurance is to protect you financially. There are certain unforeseen events that can occur preventing you from going on the trip such as a family member's death or personal injury where you will be paid back for the monetary value of the trip. Many insurance plans protect you financially by reimbursing you for missed flight connections and lost/stolen belongings. Most plans can be upgraded to include rental car coverage. You most likely do not need this, as the rental car company requires you to purchase their own insurance policy in order to cross the border into Argentina.

Just like all insurance, the greater the protection, the greater the premium. Factors such as duration of the trip, estimated monetary value of the trip, and how far in advance the trip is made prior to being insured will change the price of insurance. InsureMyTrip is a great resource to compare costs and coverages across different providers. They offer lots of resources to help you decide which coverage is best for you and understand the terms. Check with your credit card company as well to see what coverage they provide for international travel.

Packing a Backpack

There is a lot of gear you need to stuff into your pack. The position and placement of your gear will make a difference in your comfort and balance while hiking. Follow these guidelines to effectively pack:

- Cushiony stuff on the bottom! The lower compartment of your pack will be in direct contact with your back and is for soft things like the sleeping bag and pad.

- Above this soft layer should be heavier items like cookware and food. Keeping the center of gravity low on your pack will help its balance. But have that day's snack and lunch readily available for quick access upon stopping.
- Keep rain gear in a quick access compartment or at the top of your pack ready to go. Rain can come without notice, be prepared!
- Make sure all food is packed in a sealed container that doesn't risk rupture. Reinforce caps with duct tape so you don't get precious hot sauce all over your sleeping bag!

Before you start hiking, put the pack on and make sure it feels secure and well balanced. Over the course of a day, an unbalanced pack slowly causes unnecessary strain on your body.

Conclusion

Planning the trip of a lifetime in a remote region of the world requires perseverance and access to accurate information. Even with all the research you can do, there will be inevitable puzzles for you to solve. Through this guide, I hope to have cleared up uncertainties of the region, and provide you with tips to help best plan and execute your own adventure. Patagonia is a world on its own, with so much to explore. I have covered the highlights of the region that can be accomplished in three weeks or less, but those with more time and resources will find much more to experience here. There cannot be one comprehensive travel guide that answers every question and provides you with every detail to plan your trip. Seek out additional resources and perspectives. Then take all of it and make your own adventure.

Be Sure to Check Out my website at www.afineadventure.com for more guides and travel tips!

And be sure to follow me on all my social media for blog posts and tips to help you plan your next adventure!

facebook.com/afineadventure

twitter.com/afineadventure

instagram.com/a_fine_adventure/

youtube channel: A Fine Adventure

Questions or Comments? Send me a note at andyfineadventure@gmail.com

I'd love to hear your feedback, and how your adventure goes! ***Please be sure to leave a five star review on Amazon!***

About the Author

Andy Fine has been traveling the world ever since his first international trip to France in 2004. Since then he has traveled to 13 countries across five continents. As of December 2017, he has been to China, Thailand, Hong Kong, Vietnam, Japan, Australia, France, England, Greece, the British and US Virgin Islands, Canada, United States, Chile, and Argentina! His love for the outdoors and camping came from his 13 years of experience as a camper and ultimately a trips counselor at Camp Leelanau for Boys in Maple City, MI. As a certified Wilderness First Responder and trained Experiential Education leader, Andy has had great opportunities to learn what it takes to successfully trek throughout the world. Andy operates the blog, www.afineadventure.com, where he posts guides and tips for traveling the places he has been so far. When he is not traveling or camping, Andy enjoys sailing, skiing, tennis, and biking.

Trekking Patagonia: A Guide to Your Own Adventure

Emerald Lake, Banff National Park, Canada

Great Wall of China

Yosemite National Park

Lion Rock, Hong Kong

Trekking Patagonia: A Guide to Your Own Adventure

Zhanjiajie National Park, China

Pictured Rocks National Lakeshore

Cover by Andy Fine

Photos by Andy Fine, William Rohrer, and Levi Mitchell

Trekking Patagonia: A Guide to Your Own Adventure

First Edition: 2018

Made in the USA
Las Vegas, NV
21 April 2025

21174858R00073